万里长城

Customs, Traditions and Landmarks |
Non-Fiction Series

Copyright © 2022 by Level Learning, INC. and Washington Yu Ying PCS™
Original and Edited Text Copyright © 2022 by Washington Yu Ying PCS™

All rights reserved. No part of this book in whole or part may be reproduced without written permission from the publisher.

Published by Level Learning, INC.
Content Contributors:
Washington Yu Ying PCS™
Level Learning - Ya-Ching Chang

Illustrations by: Matt Austin

Leveling classification based on Level Learning standard. For full description, visit www.levellearning.com

ISBN 978-1-64040-023-8
Simplified Chinese Edition

About Level Learning:
Level Learning provides a literacy focused curriculum specifically designed for K-12 Chinese as a Second Language classrooms. Our program offers 20 levels of specific and detailed objectives, leveled texts and passages, mastery-based online assessment, and analytics to enable data-driven instruction. Level Learning reading curriculum for both literature and informational text emphasize grammar and comprehension skills to help teachers develop confident and independent Chinese language readers. The non-fiction series of books are specifically designed to support our informational text course based on multiple national standards. To learn more about our entire offering, visit www.levellearning.com.

About Washington Yu Ying PCS™:
Washington Yu Ying PCS is a Mandarin English dual language immersion International Baccalaureate (IB) World school. Yu Ying's mission is to inspire and prepare young people to create a better world by challenging them to reach their full potential in a nurturing Chinese/English educational environment. Yu Ying's comprehensive IB, dual immersion curriculum equips students with global competencies for success in the real world. As a leader in immersion education, Yu Ying is determined to advance Chinese language programs and global citizenry education by helping other schools create and strengthen their Chinese programs. For more information, email: products@washingtonyuying.org

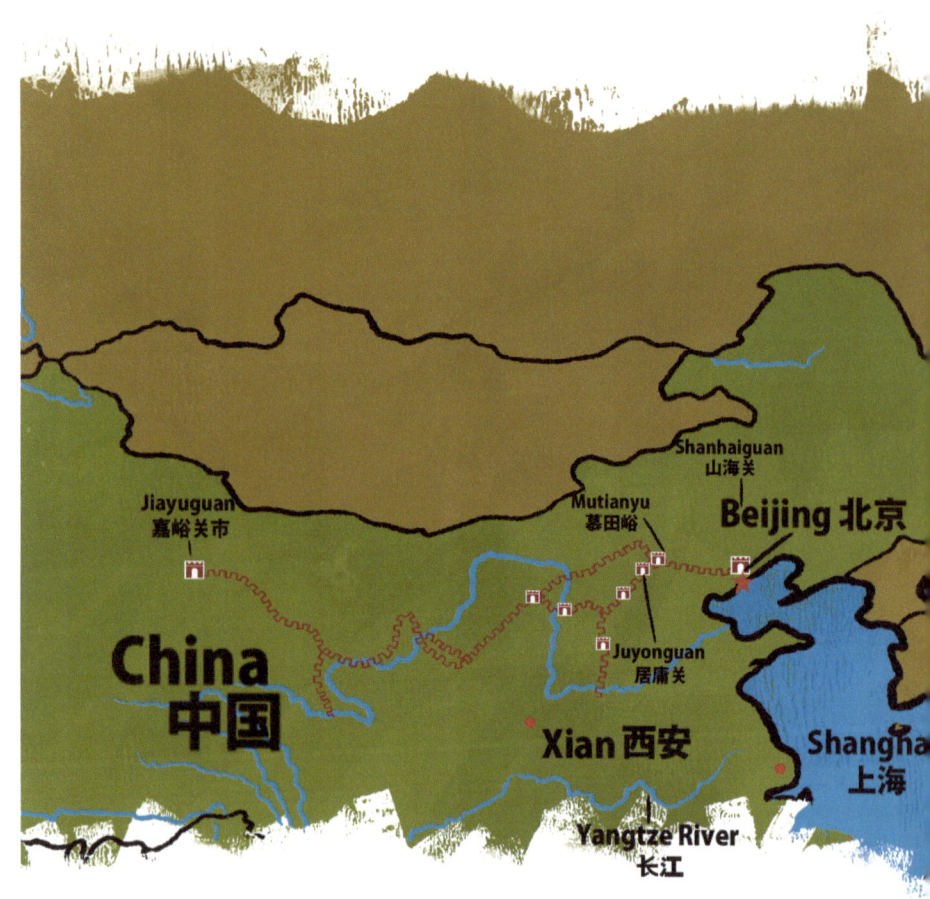

很多人都说，去中国旅行一定要去长城。因为长城不仅是一个著名的景点，而且也是中国最伟大的建筑之一。长城在中国的北方，有8851公里长，因此又被称为"万里长城"。

长城已经有两千多年的历史了。在中国历史上，很多朝代都修建过长城。虽然秦始皇不是第一个下令修建长城的君王，但是只要说到长城，人们一定会先想到秦始皇，因为他对长城的修建有非常大的影响。

在秦朝时期，一些北方的民族经常南下抢东西。后来，秦始皇下令把一些北方原有的城墙连接起来，用来保护北方的人民。有了这道长城，那些北方的民族就很难再南下，南方的人民就可以更安心地生活了。

可是在两千多年前，修建长城并不是一件简单的工作，需要很多人力和物力。所以秦始皇下令让一百多万人去北方修建长城。修建长城的工作不仅辛苦，而且北方的天气也非常寒冷。在修建长城的这段时间，很多人因为生病或受伤而死在长城下。

修建好的长城，每隔一段距离就有一个烽火台。当烽火台上的士兵看见远方有军队靠近时，白天他们就会在烽火台上点烟，晚上就会点火。其他烽火台上的士兵看到了，就知道要准备保护国家了。

在明朝时期，长城又被重新修建和加长。我们现在看到的万里长城，大多是在明朝的时候修建的。

中国有一句话是"不到长城非好汉",所以很多游客都会去登长城,做好汉。不只是中国人,也有很多外国人到中国登长城。很多外国人认为没有登过长城,就好像没有去过中国。

你登过长城吗?有机会也去登长城,做好汉吧!

Glossary

	Pinyin	English Definition
旅行	lǚ xíng	to travel
长城	cháng chéng	the Great Wall
景点	jǐng diǎn	scenic spot
建筑	jiàn zhù	building
北方	běi fāng	north
公里	gōng lǐ	kilometer
万	wàn	ten thousand
里	lǐ	a Chinese unit of length (one li is ½ kilometer)
两千	liǎng qiān	two thousand
历史	lì shǐ	history
朝代	cháo dài	dynasty
修建	xiū jiàn	to construct
秦始皇	qín shǐ huáng	The first Emperor of the Qin Dynasty
下令	xià lìng	to order
君王	jūn wáng	emperor

	Pinyin	English Definition
影响	yǐng xiǎng	influence
民族	mín zú	ethnic people
经常	jīng cháng	often
南下	nán xià	to go south
抢	qiǎng	to grab
墙	qiáng	wall
连接	lián jiē	to connect
保护	bǎo hù	to protect
难	nán	hard, difficult
安心	ān xīn	peace of mind
简单	jiǎn dān	simple
人力	rén lì	manpower
物力	wù lì	physical resources
一百多万	yì bǎi duō wàn	more than a million
辛苦	xīn kǔ	hard, exhausting
寒冷	hán lěng	cold

	Pinyin	English Definition
受伤	shòu shāng	injury
死	sǐ	to die
隔	gé	separated
距离	jù lí	distance
烽火台	fēng huǒ tái	beacon tower
士兵	shì bīng	soldier
远方	yuǎn fāng	far away
军队	jūn duì	army
靠近	kào jìn	close by, near
烟	yān	smoke
准备	zhǔn bèi	to get ready, to prepare
明朝	míng cháo	Ming Dynasty
好汉	hǎo hàn	hero, strong and courageous person
游客	yóu kè	tourist
登	dēng	to climb

www.ingramcontent.com/pod-product-compliance
Lightning Source LLC
Chambersburg PA
CBHW041221070526
44584CB00001B/47